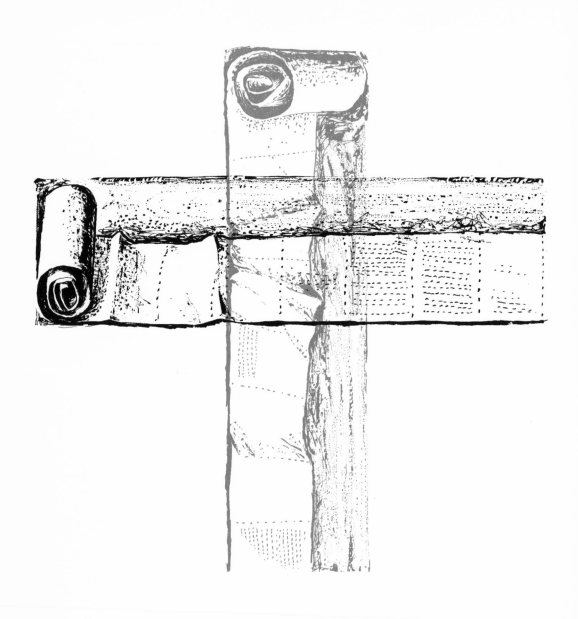

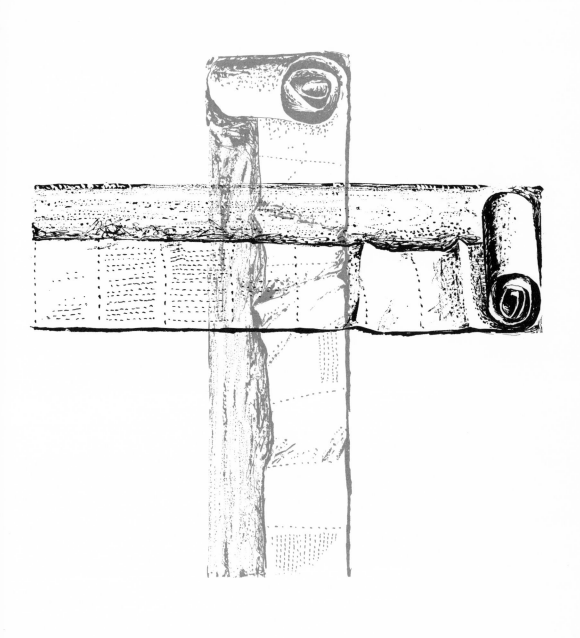

QUEST FOR THE DEAD SEA SCROLLS

When a young Bedouin goatherd found some jars containing old manuscripts in a cave in the mountains near the Dead Sea in 1947, he stumbled across the first clue to a mystery that has continued to excite scholars, archaeologists and scientists.

Ever since the first scrolls were discovered, men have been asking questions about them. Who wrote them? Why were they hidden in the depths of inaccessible caves? What connection had these crumbling manuscripts with the ruins of the nearby monastery of Qumran, where excavation has yielded fascinating details of the life of the strange people who lived there? What do the scrolls tell us of the beginnings of Christianity? Will the treasure of the copper scroll ever be found?

The two-thousand-year-old manuscripts have been the subject of numerous books for specialists, but in *Quest for the Dead Sea Scrolls* their discovery, adventures and importance are described and explained simply and clearly for the younger enthusiast of historical and archaeological riddles. In it he will find all the ingredients of a first-class detective story; a hint of smuggling; the romance of historical research; and an account of how patient men have tried to solve the puzzle of the greatest manuscript discovery of modern times.

With Illustrations by
PETER FORSTER

The John Day Company
New York

QUEST FOR THE DEAD SEA SCROLLS

by

GEOFFREY PALMER

FOR MY MOTHER

Chapter One

Spring in the mountains bordering the Dead Sea in southern Palestine is hot, and Muhammad, the Bedouin goatherd, nicknamed the Wolf, was hot too as he climbed the craggy limestone rocks. He was searching for a goat that had wandered away from the herd. He paused on a rocky ledge and wiped the sweat from his face. In the distance he could see the waters of the Dead Sea and smell its strong salty smell. Round him lay the barren wasteland called Wadi Qumran, where the only growing thing was the sun-scorched grass on the hills. Muhammad called the goat, but the animal was in search of food and took no notice. Baffled, the boy threw himself down in the shade of an overhanging ledge, pushed back the hood of his burnous and decided to cool down and rest before climbing still higher.

As he lay, his eyes wandered casually over the face of the rocks. In this region there are many caves which have sheltered many different people – hermits, outlaws and soldiers – for hundreds of years, as far back as Biblical times. Thousands of years ago the valley of the river Jordan

11

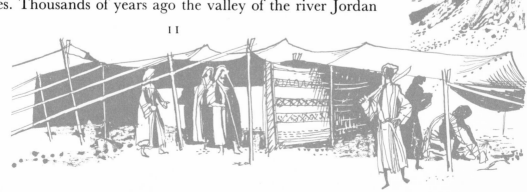

was a long lake and the present cliffs were part of the shore-line. The lake water ate into the soft rock so that caves were formed when the level of the lake fell and the water dried out. Some of the caves were not easy to see, some looked like holes in the cliff's face.

Muhammad caught his breath suddenly. There was a hole he had not noticed before, not much bigger than a man's head. He wondered whether it was indeed the entrance to a cave, or whether a trick of the sun had given a fold of the rock the appearance of a gaping hole. He picked up a stone and tossed it towards the dark patch. The stone disappeared. Muhammad expected to hear the sound of stone against stone, or the bleating of his goat which might possibly have got into the cave, but what he did hear startled him con-siderably. There was a sharp crash – the sound of breaking pottery. He was frightened. His superstitious mind immedi-ately jumped to the conclusion that he had disturbed a desert spirit that inhabited the cave.

Forgetting the lost goat he scrambled down the rocks as quickly as he could and ran back to the ragged black tents of his comrades. Muhammad was a member of the Ta'amire tribe of Bedouins who were resting at the spring of Ain Feshkha, where the only fresh water on that high plateau was to be found. The Ta'amire tribe were smugglers who

ranged the country between Bethlehem and the Dead Sea, smuggling contraband goods into Palestine from Transjordan. To avoid the customs officers at the Jordan bridge they had moved southwards and had floated their goods across the river. They were stocking up with fresh water at Ain Feshkha and waiting for the opportunity to reach the markets of Bethlehem where they could sell their goods to merchants who would not ask awkward questions.

Later that evening, when the sun had gone down, and the camels had finished their grazing and were asleep, Muhammad told the story of his adventure to an older boy and expressed his fears that he had disturbed a spirit who might do him harm. His friend laughed at the idea but was interested in the story. If there was pottery in the cave, he said, there might be treasure – treasure which would make them rich – so rich, perhaps, that they might be able to buy a motor car, like the rich Arabs in the city! Muhammad's fears gave way to greed, and the two boys decided that they would explore the cave the next day. When they had made their arrangements they pulled down the flap of their tent, lay on the ground, wrapped their burnouses round them and went to sleep.

Muhammad woke early the next morning and nudged his friend till he, too, was awake. They hastily drank some milk,

13

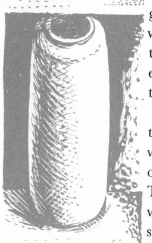

munched some dried fruit, and disappeared from the camp before their elders were stirring. The day was hot again, but the sun was not as high in the sky as it soon would be, and they were able to climb the rocks without much difficulty to where Muhammad had seen the hole in the cliff face.

They clambered over to the hole and poked their heads inside, but could see nothing. Muhammad looked at his friend. Should they venture inside? The older boy nodded, a little hesitantly, for he sensed a strangeness in the atmosphere. Everything was so still, as though the rocks were listening and waiting, holding their breaths.

With much wriggling they managed, one after the other, to get through the entrance and drop down inside. The heat was like a solid wall. The light was dim but there was enough to see what the cave was like and what it contained. At the end of a narrow passage there was a shadowy chamber, about twenty-five feet long, eight feet high and only two yards wide.

Their dark eyes glittered with anticipation. On each side of the room was a row of tall jars, made of clay. Some were whole, some crumbling, and many were broken. Pieces lay on the floor of the cave amid the debris fallen from the roof. The two boys approached the first jar expectantly. What were they going to find inside? Gold, perhaps, or precious stones. Something of great value, at least . . . They forced

14

off the tight, bowl-like lid and peered in. The jar was empty.
They looked at each other with eyes full of disappointment.
Was it worth while looking in the other jars, asked
Muhammad. His friend shrugged his shoulders. Might as
well, his gesture said.

Their persistence was rewarded. In one of the jars they
found what at first sight they thought to be some cloth-
covered bundles. They pulled them out and turned them
over curiously. The bundles were brittle and crumbly and
gave off a disagreeable smell that got up their noses and made
them cough. Muhammad pulled away at the linen cloth and
exposed a roll of smooth brown leather. Whatever could it be?
Nothing very valuable, that was certain. Other jars contained similar rolls with a black waxy surface, but of gold
or precious stones there was no sign.

After a brief discussion they decided to take some of the
bundles back with them to their encampment to show their
chief. They put them in one of the empty jars and hoisted it
out of the cave and into the welcome sunlight. Thankfully
they breathed the clean-smelling air. With frequent rests
they carried their burden back to the camp.

In their tent, with a circle of watching Bedouins around
and the chief looking on sternly, they told their story and
unwrapped the largest bundle. The linen cover was coated

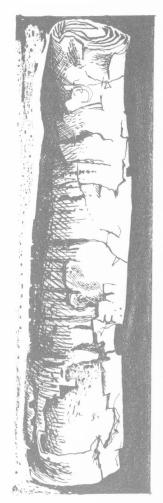

15

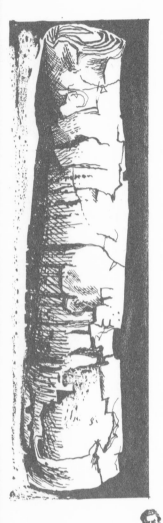

with pitch or wax. Inside there were thin sheets of leather that had been sewn together and which contained parallel lines of writing. The boys unrolled the scroll. It seemed to stretch from one end of the tent to the other!

The chief examined the strange inscriptions on the leather sheets. He retreated, shaking his head. He had never seen anything like it before. The language was certainly not Arabic. He would have recognized that, even though he could neither read nor write. None of the other Bedouins could help to solve the mystery. They decided that the scrolls were probably very old and that possibly they might be able to sell them for a small sum in Bethlehem. Somebody might want the leather, though they could not think to what use it might be put, being so fragile. Muhammad hoped that they might get enough money for the scrolls to make up for the lost goat!

After the first excitement the Bedouins lost interest in the scrolls. The time was 1947, soon after the ending of the Second World War. Many goods were still in short supply and there were always people who were willing to pay a high price for them. Being so active in this illegal business the Ta'amire tribe had little time to think of the musty old pieces of leather. When they eventually reached Bethlehem they went to the market place to sell their milk and cheese openly and their contraband articles secretly.

16

They showed the scrolls first to a Muslim Sheikh. He was not very interested. He thought the mysterious language was probably Syriac and recommended them to go to a man called Khalil Eskander, usually known as Kando, who kept a general shop and a cobbler's shop next door. Kando was a Syrian and a Christian. He belonged to a branch of the Christian Church called the Syrian Orthodox, and the Sheikh thought that he might recognize the script.

Kando took the scrolls and said he would let the Bedouins know later what he had found out about them. He pushed them into a corner of the shop and promptly forgot all about them. Some days later he noticed the dusty bundles. The leather might do for repairing shoes, he thought, and picked one of them up. He examined the writing. No, he did not recognize it. It meant nothing to him. When a merchant friend, another Syrian Christian called George Isaiah, from Jerusalem, called to see him, they discussed the matter. George Isaiah wasn't at all sure that the scrolls were worthless. He thought that it would be a good idea to give them over to an expert on old manuscripts and suggested that the next time Kando went to Jerusalem on business he should take one of them to the Archbishop Samuel, head of the Syrian Orthodox Monastery of Saint Mark, in the old part of the city. The monastery owned a library of ancient Syriac

manuscripts, and George Isaiah said they would surely be able to identify the language of the scrolls there.

This Kando did. The Archbishop Samuel (his full title was the Metropolitan Mar Athanasius Yeshue Samuel) was very interested in the find. He broke off a small piece of the scroll and burned it. The smell told him that it was either leather or parchment. He declared that the language was not Syriac, but Hebrew, though he was unable to read it. He knew that nobody had settled in the Wadi Qumran wasteland since early Christian times and that if the story about the scrolls being found in a Dead Sea cave were true then they must be about two thousand years old and therefore very valuable. So he told Kando that he would buy the scrolls, and Kando went back to Bethlehem promising to get in touch with Muhammad the Wolf and the other Bedouins.

But the Ta'amire tribe was on its travels again and several weeks went by before the Bedouins returned to the market place of Bethlehem. One Saturday in July Kando was able to telephone the Archbishop that they had arrived and were willing to do business. Three Bedouins would take four more scrolls with them, he said.

The day came when the Archbishop expected his visitors. They did not arrive during the morning and the Archbishop thought that perhaps they had been delayed. So he went to his midday meal, forgetting to tell the priest on duty at the gate of the monastery about the expected tribesmen. While the Archbishop was away George Isaiah and the Bedouins, including Muhammad, arrived at the monastery. The priest who met them at the door was rather scared at their sinister appearance and refused to let them inside. George Isaiah showed him the scrolls but the priest was not impressed. He declared that the Archbishop would have no use for the dusty old manuscripts, especially as they were written in Hebrew and not Syriac. No, the Archbishop would not want them . . . He advised them to find a Jewish buyer.

The disappointed Bedouins left the monastery gates and went back to a square near the Jaffa Gate, in the Arab section of the city. There they found a Jewish merchant who offered them a good price for the scrolls but said he had not got the money with him and would have to get it from his office, which was in the new part of the city, the Jewish section.

Now in the summer of 1947 the Jewish part of Jerusalem was under martial law and people were not allowed to travel freely. Jews and Arabs were bitter enemies and the Jews hated the British who, they thought, were siding with the Arabs. Jews had murdered British soldiers and the British had been hanging Jews. Bombs were thrown and

mines laid. Palestine was a sad, bitter country, full of hatred, terrorism and misunderstanding. George Isaiah managed to persuade the Bedouins that the Jewish merchant was playing a trick on them and that if they were caught in the Jewish section they would be robbed and arrested, and might not even escape with their lives. He told them too of the law that said that newly discovered antiquities had to be reported to the Government. The Bedouins, after thinking of all that might happen to them, and not liking the prospect, agreed to leave their scrolls with George and he promised he would try again to see the Archbishop.

Two weeks later George, Kando and the Bedouins trudged through the hot dusty streets of Jerusalem and arrived again at the Monastery of Saint Mark. This time they were not turned away at the gates but let in by a very apologetic priest. The Archbishop, dressed in a black robe with big sleeves, a black satin hat shaped like an onion, his black beard quivering with eagerness, met them with dignified pleasure. He examined the five scrolls they had brought – though two of them were parts of a single manuscript which had broken apart – and said he would buy them all, including one which was in such a bad state that it seemed it would be impossible to open it.

20

After much bargaining the Bedouins went away with a large sum of British money, very satisfied with their transaction. Muhammad grinned widely as they left the monastery. He regarded himself as the hero of the hour. After all, if he had not gone searching for the lost goat, and if he had not by chance thrown a stone into the cave, none of this would have happened.

Chapter Two

ONE OF THE first things that the Archbishop Samuel did after buying the Hebrew manuscripts was to check up on the story the Bedouins had told him. During the second week in August he sent one of his priests, Father Yusef, to the cave, together with George Isaiah, the Syrian merchant, and with Muhammad as their guide. When Muhammad had shown the two men the entrance he was given a good tip and sent away to rejoin his tribe.

It was late when the priest and the merchant arrived at the opening of the cave and they decided to spend the night inside. The heat was stifling and they had a very uncomfortable time during their exploration. They found little of any value – one undamaged but empty jar, bits of broken pottery, pieces of linen wrappings and fragments of scrolls. They considered trying to take back the whole jar with them, but decided that it was too heavy to carry in the intense summer heat. So they returned to the monastery with nothing to show for their journey.

The Archbishop was disappointed but resigned. Next he thought he would try to find out the probable age and value of the scrolls he already had.

23

There were many archaeologists in and around Jerusalem, an ancient city of great religious and historical importance, and two people the Archbishop tried to see were Mr G. L. Harding, who was employed by the Jordan Government to study old relics, and Father Roland de Vaux, who belonged to the French Bible and Archaeology School. But Mr Harding was too busy to see the Archbishop and the French priest was away.

He had better luck with a famous Biblical scholar from Holland, Father van der Ploeg, who was a visitor at the French Bible School. The Dutchman examined the largest scroll and said immediately that it was the Old Testament Book of Isaiah – a very early copy. This first hint that the scrolls might be of great age spurred the Archbishop on to greater efforts. He tried to study the Hebrew language himself but, being a member of the Syrian Church, found the task difficult. All visitors to the monastery were asked what they thought of the scrolls. Most of them said they were worthless and pooh-poohed the Archbishop's suggestion that they might be anything up to two thousand years old.

In September he took the scrolls to Syria, to the Patriarch of Antioch. Three hundred years old, said the Patriarch. He tried to see the Professor of Hebrew at the American University of Beirut but he was away on holiday in America.

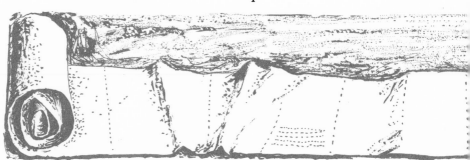

He returned to Jerusalem, still determined not to give up his search for someone who could tell him the truth about the scrolls. Then he was introduced to an antique dealer and Hebrew scholar named Wechsler. Mr Wechsler, too, was unable to believe that the scrolls were as old as the Archbishop hoped. He suggested that they had been stolen from a Palestine synagogue during riots that had taken place between Jews and Arabs in 1929.

The Archbishop stuck to his guns that he had come into possession of some very ancient holy books. Mr Wechsler shook his head but declared that if the table the scrolls were resting on were a box and that box full of pound notes it would still not be big enough to hold their full value – *if* what the Archbishop hoped was true. He did agree, however, that one scroll was the text of Isaiah and that it was slightly different from the text they were used to.

One day the Archbishop had a visitor, a Jewish physician named Dr Maurice Brown, who had come to see him about renting a building that the monastery owned. Of course Dr Brown, like every other visitor, had to hear the story of the scrolls. He was very interested and was sorry that he himself did not have the knowledge to help. But he immediately informed the President of the Hebrew University in Jerusalem, Dr Judah L. Magnes, and the President sent two of his staff

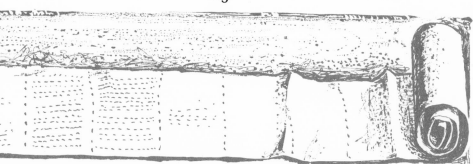

to the monastery. They examined the scrolls and asked for permission to photograph part of one of them. The Archbishop agreed willingly – but the photographer never turned up, nor did the two men. This was probably because relations between the Jews and the Arabs had become so bitter that Jerusalem was now a battleground. Guerilla activity became widespread and there was confusion everywhere. In addition, the Hebrew University's chief archaeologist, Professor E. L. Sukenik, was away in America and did not hear of the manuscripts until he returned to Palestine at the end of November.

So the Archbishop Samuel was frustrated again. It seemed as though he would never make any progress. All his efforts had led to dead ends and blind alleys. He did not know what to do next. It had been suggested to him that he should send parts of the manuscripts to antique dealers in Europe and the United States, but he was reluctant to let them out of his hands. There were so many experts locally – surely one of them, sometime, somehow, would be able to put his mind at rest!

The story now takes an odd twist, away from Archbishop Samuel and Saint Mark's Monastery.

When Professor Sukenik, of the Hebrew University, did return from the United States he heard that a dealer in

Bethlehem had some old manuscripts he might be interested in. This dealer turned out to be Kando . . . who had bought up the remaining scrolls from the Bedouins. Professor Sukenik saw some fragments in Kando's shop, after a difficult journey to Bethlehem on a November day just before savage hostilities broke out between Arabs and Jews, and he took three manuscripts back with him to Jerusalem, one of them in three pieces, and a number of fragments. In December he bought another scroll in bad condition. But he still had not heard of those in the possession of the Archbishop . . .

The more Professor Sukenik thought about and studied these ancient writings the more his excitement grew. He held a Press Conference one afternoon at the offices of the Jewish Agency, and announced that he believed he had discovered the most ancient Hebrew manuscripts ever known – probably written a hundred or two hundred years before the birth of Christ. While he was telling the reporters his story shells were bursting all around the office. One reporter fainted, but the Professor talked on, undisturbed by the banging. Gradually all who heard him were impressed by his enthusiasm and forgot the danger they were in.

There was still no connection between the Professor and the Archbishop. Neither knew that the other owned precious

documents from the same source, the cave near the Dead Sea. But the two strands of the story are getting closer . . .

It was not until February, 1948, that the Archbishop's patience was rewarded. Almost a year had gone by since Muhammad the Wolf had thrown his stone and heard the crash of breaking pottery – a year in which the Archbishop had met with nothing but difficulties and disappointments. But now things began to happen quickly.

A monk of Saint Mark's Monastery, Brother Butros Sowmy, remembered that he had, many years before, been made welcome at the American School of Oriental Research in Jerusalem when he had visited it. Would that be a good place to try to get information about the scrolls? he asked his Archbishop. The Archbishop agreed to let him take the scrolls there, but without hope that they would get any help.

Brother Sowmy telephoned the American School. The Director, Dr Millar Burrows, was away in Iraq, he was told. Was it to be the same old story? Everyone away or just not interested? The monk persisted. Was there anyone else he and his brother Ibrahim could see? Yes, there was Dr John C. Trever, who was in charge while Dr Burrows was away. He would see them.

The next day the two monks descended on Dr Trever, carrying the scrolls wrapped in newspaper in an old suitcase.

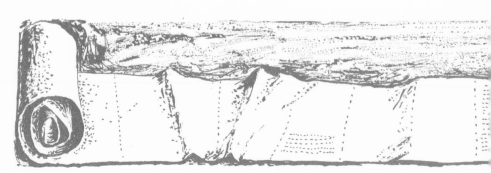

They unrolled them onto a table. In silence Dr Trever compared the old Hebrew writing on them with samples of other manuscripts by flashing colored slides onto a wall screen. One slide was a picture from a ninth century manuscript now in the British Museum. Another was of a fragment of papyrus called the Nash Papyrus, housed in the University Library at Cambridge and thought to be nearly two thousand years old. The scripts of the scrolls and the Nash Papyrus were strikingly alike! Dr Trever declared that the monks *had* brought him a scroll of Isaiah and that it *was* really very very old – in fact, probably the oldest manuscript of the Bible ever known! It would be difficult to decide who was the more thrilled, Dr Trever or the monks – or the Archbishop Samuel when he heard the news and knew that his optimism had been justified.

Although Europeans had not been allowed in the Old City of Jerusalem for months, Dr Trever and his Arab secretary managed to get through the narrow winding streets without too much trouble, though there were armed guards everywhere and the sound of rifle shots in the distance. They saw the Archbishop, who gave them permission for the scrolls to be photographed. He was so delighted that his theory seemed to be coming true that he agreed to take the scrolls himself to the American School the next day and watch the work being done.

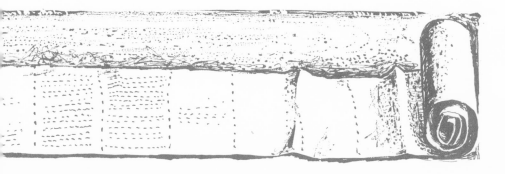

On Saturday, February 21st, the photographing began. It was a difficult task as the electricity current kept failing and the supply of film was scanty and of poor quality, and it was impossible to buy any more in that war-torn city. One of the scrolls was so badly damaged and brittle that Dr Trever could not unroll it. He could not risk breaking the parchment into pieces so it was left undisturbed. He hoped that later on the leather could be softened by chemicals.

Dr Trever and another scholar, Dr William Brownlee, worked hard at the long and tedious job. The broken pieces of each scroll had to be carefully fitted together and then stuck. At the end of the first day two complete scrolls had been photographed, the Book of Isaiah and the Book of Habakkuk. The Archbishop and Brother Sowmy returned to the monastery, well pleased with the way things were going. The two Americans, after a quick meal, developed the negatives of the first day's work and made prints.

The photographing went on all over the weekend. Because the film they used was so old the pictures came out dark and blurred, but Dr Trever and Dr Brownlee pressed on in haste, doing as well as they could with such poor materials. The third scroll they worked on was in two parts. It is now known as the Manual of Discipline and describes the way of life of a group of Jews who lived in a settlement on the western shore of the Dead Sea two thousand years ago.

Prints of columns of the Isaiah scroll were sent by air mail to Dr W. F. Albright of the Johns Hopkins University in Baltimore, one of the greatest living archaeologists. How old is this writing? Dr Trever asked him. Are these manuscripts really ancient? Or are they forgeries?

Dr Albright's reply brought relief and joy to the scholars of the Oriental School of Research. Dr Albright had no doubt that the script was older than that of the Nash Papyrus. Around 100 B.C., he thought. He had no doubt that it was genuine. They had on their hands the greatest manuscript discovery of modern times. It was absolutely incredible, he finished.

In spite of all difficulties and doubts it was now certain that the Dead Sea Scrolls contained the oldest manuscripts of the Bible ever known. Excitement ran high in the Oriental School, in Saint Mark's Monastery, and in every place where scholars heard about them.

Chapter Three

WE MUST NOW return to Professor Sukenik of the Hebrew University and the scrolls that he had bought from the Bedouins through Kando. There were three of them. One was another copy of the Book of Isaiah, though not as complete as the one that the Archbishop had bought. Another had the title The War of the Sons of Light with the

18544

SYRIA
Sea of Galilee
ISRAEL
Jerusalem
Jordan
JORDAN
Bethlehem
Dead Sea

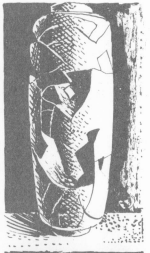

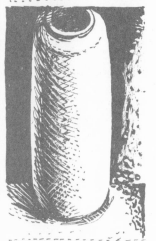

Sons of Darkness. The third consisted of Psalms of Thanksgiving, similar to the psalms we are familiar with. When
Professor Sukenik heard that the Archbishop Samuel had
some similar manuscripts he wanted very much to see them,
naturally, and compare them with his own. But he lived in the
New City and Saint Mark's Monastery was in the Old City,
and it was impossible to get from one part to the other
because of the fighting. So he had to give up the idea – tem-
porarily, he hoped. He worked on his own scrolls, photographing, translating, and writing articles about them. He
had a theory that the Qumran cave had been a *genizah*, a
room in which old manuscripts were stored – those that were
of no further use to a monastery or a synagogue but were
too sacred to be destroyed.

In January, 1948, he received a letter from a Mr Kiraz, a
member of the Syrian Orthodox community in the Old
City, asking to meet him in the Y.M.C.A. building as he
wanted the Professor's advice about some old manuscripts
he knew of. Would that be possible?

The Y.M.C.A. happened to be in a neutral area of Jerusalem and Professor Sukenik was able to get a pass. He therefore arranged to see this mysterious Mr Kiraz. When they
met one dark night they exchanged information, the Professor heard all about the Archbishop's scrolls and was able

36

to examine three of them by torchlight. His interest reached a high pitch – would the Archbishop sell them to the Hebrew University? Mr Kiraz thought it would be possible. He left the three scrolls with the professor and said he could keep them for two days. The professor hurried back to the University and copied out several columns of the Isaiah scroll, which he later published. Mr Kiraz' mission and offer to sell seems to have been done without the Archbishop's knowledge, and though another meeting was arranged it never took place and the deal dropped through, though, of course, the Archbishop's scrolls were returned to the monastery.

The Archbishop was making his own arrangements – it was at this time that Brother Sowmy got in touch with the American School of Oriental Research and met Dr Trever. He decided not to sell the scrolls just then but to allow the American School to publish their contents. But he did promise that the Hebrew University would be given the first chance to buy them when they were eventually offered for sale. The Archbishop wanted to get the best price he could for the scrolls and he felt that, when the hostilities between Jews and Arabs were over, he would be more certain of their proper value. Professor Sukenik was very disappointed at the Archbishop's decision and had to content himself with further study on the three scrolls the Hebrew University had already bought.

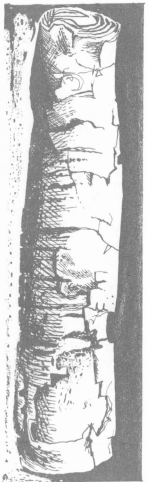

At the end of February, when Dr Millar Burrows, the Director of the American School of Oriental Research, returned from his journey to Iraq, and heard about what had been going on, he became as enthusiastic as all the other people who had been connected with the scrolls. He told Archbishop Samuel that he thought the Isaiah scroll was the oldest known manuscript of any book of the Bible. The Archbishop was so impressed that he sent his scrolls out of Palestine to a place of safety, but not before he had given Dr Trever a fragment of one of them.

It was as well that he did. The fighting in Palestine grew fiercer. The Arabs shelled the Old City and Saint Mark's Monastery caught fire and suffered great damage. Brother Sowmy was killed. Nobody, nothing was safe.

So early in 1949 the Archbishop left his country and sailed for the United States, taking his precious manuscripts with him. He met Dr Burrows, who had also by this time left Palestine and returned to Yale University, and handed over the scrolls to the Headquarters of the American School for three years.

There Dr Trever and Dr Brownlee continued their work and took on the task of preparing the translations of the manuscripts for publication. At the end of the three years the Archbishop, who had stayed in America all this time, insisted

38

on taking the scrolls back, even though it had proved impossible to unroll one of them and no one had any idea of its contents. The Archbishop started to try to sell them to American universities and libraries. For a long time he was unsuccessful. Some people were put off by the rumor that the price the Archbishop was asking was a million dollars. Others were not sure who the real owner of the scrolls was and did not want to get involved in a law suit; or they were suspicious of the way they had been removed from Palestine without the knowledge of the Government.

The scrolls were shown to the public in several places but still no definite buyer came forward. It was not until 1955 that it was officially announced that the scrolls had been bought for the Government of Israel by the son of Professor Sukenik. His name was Yigael Yadin, and he was an archaeologist, though at that time a general in the Israeli army. While he was in the United States in 1954 on a lecture tour he received a telephone call from a journalist friend who told him that an advertisement in the Wall Street Journal offered four Dead Sea Scrolls for sale. A banker friend conducted the negotiations with the Archbishop, and eventually they agreed on a quarter of a million dollars as a fair price.

The scrolls travelled in a black trunk from the Waldorf-Astoria Hotel to the Israel Consulate. General Yigael Yadin then began to plan for their return to Israel. They were sent by air from New York, each scroll in a different plane. It had taken seven years for them to travel the short journey from the Dead Sea cave to their last home at the Hebrew University in Jerusalem. There they were put in a specially built museum with the three that Professor Sukenik had bought many years before, and there was great joy among the Hebrew scholars.

The two strands of the first part of this amazing story had come together and were intertwined. Professor Sukenik himself, however, did not live to see his dream come true. He died in 1953, broken-hearted by the death of his younger son, a fighter-pilot in the Israeli army.

The Archbishop Samuel remained in America, living comfortably in a small cottage in New Jersey, visiting other Syrian Christians and making plans to build a small cathedral. The money he had received for the scrolls was all sent to Syria to help in building and keeping up schools and churches.

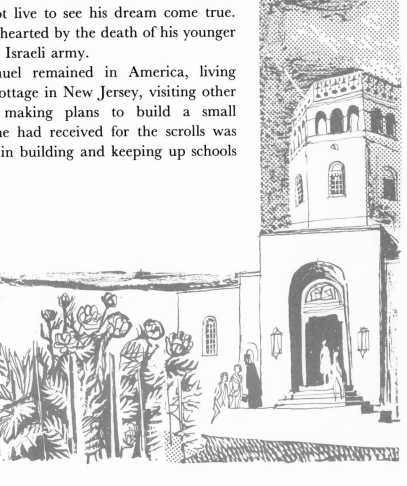

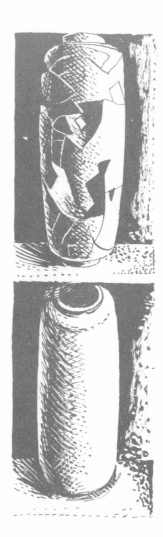

Chapter Four

SEVERAL YEARS WERE spanned in the last chapter in describing how the first scrolls were finally united in the Hebrew University, and of the efforts of Professor Sukenik and his son General Yigael Yadin to bring this about. It is now necessary to return in time to the year 1949 to follow the quest for the Dead Sea Scrolls from another angle, and with other people involved.

The war between the Jews and the Arabs had officially ended though there was still a good deal of unrest. Two men who were very briefly mentioned in the early stages of the adventure now play a greater part. They were Mr G. L. Harding, of the Jordan Department of Antiquities, and Father Roland de Vaux, of the French Bible and Archaeology School, both of whom the Archbishop had failed to get in touch with when he first bought the scrolls from the Bedouins.

In February, 1949, knowing much more of what had happened, they visited the cave where the scrolls had been found and a number of other caves near the Ain Feshkha spring. They stayed in the district nearly a month, collecting small pieces of manuscripts, broken pottery, pieces of a Roman lamp and a cooking pot.

The Bedouins, now aware that the manuscripts they had discovered two years before were valuable, began to look in other caves in the neighborhood, and by the end of 1951 they had collected handfuls of crumbled papyrus and parchment, some a few square inches in area, others no bigger than a finger nail. These they took and sold to Father de Vaux. He examined them and found that some of the fragments were in Hebrew, others in Aramaic and Greek. Though the Bedouins were willing to sell their finds they would not tell him where they had found them, in case their illegal activities might attract the attention of the police.

So Father de Vaux and Mr Harding decided that it was time a thorough and well-organized search was made of as much of the region as possible. Some of the tribesmen were officially employed to help so that they would have no qualms about disclosing the source of any material they found. In 1952 there was an expedition to the caves of Wadi Murabba'at, about eleven miles south of the Wadi Qumran, an equally wild place of rocky hills. There a rich store of fragments and coins were discovered. Some of the fragments were from scrolls written in Biblical times, others were later, from the second century A.D. These caves had been occupied at several different times. Most of the coins and manuscript fragments were from the time of the Jewish

44

Revolt against Rome (A.D. 132–135). There were only a few short bits of books of the Bible.

Soon after this expedition another one was made to explore still further the Wadi Qumran district. Father de Vaux was again associated with it, but Mr Harding had been replaced by Professor Reed, who was serving as Director of the American School of Oriental Research for a year. Altogether two hundred and sixty-seven caves and crevices were entered. About forty caves were found to contain pottery and other objects, and in twenty-five of them the pottery was of the same kind that Muhammad had found five years earlier in the first cave. Thousands of manuscript fragments included parts of the Books of Leviticus, Exodus, Ruth, Isaiah, Jeremiah and the Psalms. It was becoming clear that a whole library had been hidden in these caves. But who had the library belonged to? And why had the scrolls been hidden? There *was* a clue to the answers to these questions, but it was faint and indefinite.

Of very great interest was the discovery of two scrolls made of copper, not of papyrus, one of them containing two sections rolled up as one. It was clear from the outside that they contained writing, but they could not be unrolled because the copper had oxidized. It was not until 1956 that experts of the Manchester College of Technology, under the

direction of Professor H. Wright Baker, succeeded in a very difficult and complicated task.

They filled in the loose spaces of the scroll with plaster of paris, ran a spindle through the center, coated the outside with a plastic composition, and baked it. The scroll turned on the spindle like meat roasting on a spit, and at the same time it moved on rails under a very fine circular saw. The saw cut narrow strips lengthways from the outermost layer, and the scroll was turned after each cut. The coating and baking were repeated as often as necessary until the whole scroll had been cut in strips. Each strip was removed, cleaned and finally photographed. All this was finished in April, 1956.

Twelve columns of Hebrew text were revealed, and when the text had been translated it was found to contain directions to the hiding places of hoards of treasure. Here was romance and excitement – over sixty places in Palestine where vast treasures, gold, silver, aromatics and scrolls, were said to be hidden! Father J. T. Milik published a French translation of the text in 1959, and Dr John Allegro an English version in 1960. The two translations differ a great deal, unfortunately, and in any case the directions were too vague for exact identification of the places to be made. Scholars are still hoping that the mystery will be solved in time.

The total quantity of treasure mentioned in the scroll

comes to nearly a hundred tons of gold, silver and other precious materials. It is supposed to be hidden in places nearly fifty miles apart, but mostly near Jerusalem, and up to eighteen feet underground. It is in, or near, tombs, cisterns and canals. If found, its value would be hundreds of thousands of dollars.

Who could have possessed such a treasure? Who hid it, and when? Was such treasure ever buried? It seems very doubtful. Many scholars think it is imaginary. They think that the scroll was the work of a hermit, perhaps, who lived in a cave. Other scholars think that the scroll may be the account of the wealth given up by members of a religious community who lived nearby. Such men would give up their riches when they entered the order, and it might have been pooled and hidden as the document suggests. Or was it Temple treasure, hidden from the Romans when they attacked Jerusalem?

Perhaps the most widely held theory is that the copper scroll preserves an ancient tradition concerning the treasures of the first Temple in Jerusalem which was destroyed by King Nebuchadnezzar of Babylon in 587 B.C. The tradition would be kept alive by priests and handed down through hundreds of years like a folk story. In that case the story would have a core of truth but would have all sorts of exaggerated details added to it.

Nothing can be proved about this mysterious treasure until an agreed translation is available and excavations made at some of the places which might be identified. Perhaps even then archaeologists will be at a loss, for some of these places had been abandoned and were uninhabited even in Roman times. It will be disappointing, of course, if the treasure turns out to be nothing but a story, but such disappointments are all part of the life of an archaeologist, and he is used to being unable to find answers to many of his problems.

From 1952 onwards there were further explorations and further discoveries. Bedouins found another cave in 1956, a little to the north of the original cave. It was the eleventh to contain important discoveries. This one held five almost complete scrolls, including part of the Book of Leviticus and a scroll of Psalms. Bedouins still continue to find fragments, and Dr Allegro has reported that Bedouin tribesmen have received about $280,000 for the bits and pieces they have discovered during the last fifteen years!

The search still goes on. At any time new discoveries of great historical value may be made, discoveries that could shed new light on what happened in Biblical times. Muhammad little knew of the gigantic snowball he had started.

Chapter Five

How is it possible to be sure that the Dead Sea Scrolls are as old as most scholars now think they are? How can archaeologists prove the age of the relics they discover? Until recently mistakes were frequently made because so much was guesswork. But nowadays, by various scientific methods and tests, we can calculate the age of very old things much more accurately, and sometimes to within a very few years. And it is surprising how often earlier guesses have turned out to be approximately correct.

When the news of the discovery of the Dead Sea Scrolls was first announced there were many people who were unwilling to believe that they could be dated to a time as long ago as two thousand years. All sorts of other dates were suggested and a great deal of heated argument took place. Gradually, however, it subsided and now there is general agreement on the subject.

Professor Sukenik and a French author, Henri Del Medico, considered that the cave in which the scrolls were deposited was a *genizah* – a place for manuscripts unfit to be used. Such manuscripts could not by law be destroyed, and it was the custom in Biblical times to set them aside and after a time burn them ceremoniously. Against that theory is the

fact that manuscripts were put in a *genizah* one or two at a time, and not carefully wrapped up and put in jars, as the scrolls had been. The scrolls had evidently formed part of a very large library, and had probably been hidden to keep them safe when their owners were in great danger and forced to leave their homes. When the discovery of scrolls in many caves had been made it was clear that the library had contained hundreds of manuscripts, including several copies of some of the books, and had been broken up and distributed among the caves for greater safety.

But how old are the scrolls? If, as some scholars thought, they go no further back than the Middle Ages, then they have nothing to do with the beginnings of Christianity. If they belong to the second or third century A.D. they are interesting, but not particularly important. But if they belong to a time either just before or just after the Christian era, then they are of enormous importance in throwing light on the life and times, thoughts and views of early Christianity. As soon as it was known that one of the scrolls described a community with a strong resemblance to the first Christian churches, and another spoke of a Teacher of Righteousness who may have been the founder of this community, then it became very important to discover exactly how old the scrolls were, in order to see whether their contents could give further information about the time during which Jesus had lived.

Two of the chief opponents of an early dating were Professor G. R. Driver in England and Professor Solomon Zeitlin in America. Their theories were attacked by Professor Albright, of Johns Hopkins University, a great expert on ancient Hebrew writings, and Dr S. A. Birnbaum, among others, who were always convinced of an early date.

The pottery found in the first cave was one of the chief things that archaeologists had as clues, and they set to work to fix a date for its manufacture. Their final findings place it as belonging to the first two-thirds of the first century A.D. The manuscripts, however, were older than the pottery, and the texts copied in them were older still.

Another material to be studied was the cloth which had been wrapped round the manuscripts. It was badly decomposed, but a microscopic examination of the fiber showed that it was linen, and had been made from flax grown in Palestine.

Then the Carbon-14 process was used. This was a method invented by Professor Willard F. Libby, an American of the University of California, who was awarded a Nobel Prize in 1960. He knew that radio-active carbon comes from outer space and is absorbed by all living plants and animals. After they die the radioactivity created by the carbon lessens at a

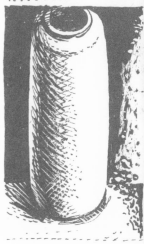

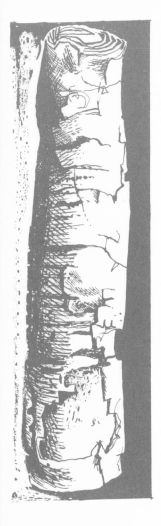

rate that can be measured. He discovered that in 5,700 years it has been reduced by a half, and when the remaining radio-active carbon in anything which has lived is measured by sensitive instruments it is possible to find how long ago it died, within a margin of error of about 5 per cent to 10 per cent.

During the Carbon-14 test the sample is burned to pure carbon and what is left is measured with a very sensitive radiation meter which works on the principle of a Geiger counter. When the test was applied to a piece of the linen in 1950 the measurements showed that it was made sometime between 167 B.C. and A.D. 233.

The leather of the manuscripts was tested at the University of Leeds and found to be from young goats and lambs. Dr Plenderleith, of the British Museum, found that the ink was a non-metallic composition, and as ink containing iron was not generally used by the Jews before the second or third century A.D. this was another useful pointer in the right direction.

The palaeographer then took over the work of the archaeologist. Palaeography means the study of the kind of script used by the writer of a manuscript, and experts in the ancient Hebrew language studied the scrolls and gave their opinions. Different forms of each letter of the alphabet found in different documents at various times had to be

54

carefully compared, because styles of writing have changed through the years in the way that styles of building and clothing and pottery have. The experts could not give the exact year in which a manuscript was written, but they could calculate the period to which it belonged to within twenty-five or fifty years.

Dr Birnbaum compared the writing of the scrolls with that of other documents, such as a tenth century A.D. manuscript in Hebrew kept in Leningrad, a ninth century one in the British Museum, a piece from the Cambridge University Library of the seventh century, a fifth century Hebrew letter, an Egyptian papyrus of the fourth century, and a fragment of the third century found in Mesopotamia, among others. None of these scripts resembled those of the Dead Sea Scrolls in any way that would indicate that the latter were written during any of those centuries.

There are enough Hebrew writings of the third and second centuries to show that they, too, are of a later date than the scrolls.

When we come to still earlier times, as far back as 200 B.C., there are no manuscripts with an exact date with which to compare the cave manuscripts, but there are inscriptions and names scratched on stone chests, tombs and boundary stones, and such scripts are more like that of the scrolls than

55

any of those of later times. The greatest number of similarities with the scrolls was found in the Nash papyrus, a small fragment written in Hebrew and containing the Ten Commandments, which belongs to the Cambridge University Library and is believed to have been written in the second century B.C.

As a result of all the work done on the scripts the palaeographer believes that the scrolls could have been written at various times between about 300 B.C. and A.D. 70, and all the other evidence such as the choice of words, the spelling and the grammar, the joining up of letters and the marks on the manuscripts, seems to bear this out. The oldest of the almost complete scrolls, the Isaiah scroll bought by the Archbishop Samuel, was written in approximately 100 B.C. The Manual of Discipline comes from the same period. The Habakkuk Commentary is about seventy-five years later, and the Lamech scroll, the War of the Sons of Light with the Sons of Darkness and the Thanksgiving Psalms were all written probably in the first fifty years after the birth of Christ.

Now that the age of the scrolls has been settled, the next thing we must ask ourselves is – who wrote them? Where and how did these people live? Why were the scrolls put in the caves and abandoned? What is the mystery behind them?

The answers to these questions lead us to more exciting discoveries that were made in the Dead Sea region soon after the first manuscripts had been found, discoveries that linked the scrolls to men who had lived a strange life in strange times, in a building the ruins of which can still be seen about three-quarters of a mile from the cave where Muhammad flung his famous stone.

Chapter Six

THE RUINS OF Khirbet Qumran, buried on the shore between the cliffs and the Dead Sea, with only a bit of stone wall showing above the ground, have been known for a long time, and also the cemetery connected with them, which contains over a thousand graves. It was thought that the ruins were those of a Roman fortress, and little interest had been taken in them by archaeologists. In 1873 a French explorer found that the graves contained the remains of corpses buried four feet deep and covered over with bricks made from unbaked clay. The graves lay in a north to south direction, and so could not contain the bodies of Muslims, who are always buried in an east/west direction. But there was nothing to indicate that they were Christian graves either, and the whole thing was a rather unimportant mystery.

A Roman writer, Pliny the Elder, writing in about A.D. 70, mentioned that he had seen a monastery on the western shore of the Dead Sea belonging to a religious sect called the Essenes. After the first Dead Sea Scrolls had been found, and scholars were beginning to wonder where they had been written, Professor A. Dupont-Sommer, of the University of Paris, argued that the Khirbet Qumran ruins were very

59

likely the ruins of the monastery that Pliny had written about. The manuscripts could not have been written in the caves in which they had been found, and both Jericho and Jerusalem were too far away for it to be likely that the scrolls had been brought from a city to these caves in the wilderness.

In 1949 it was decided that the ruins ought to be excavated, and Mr G. L. Harding and Father de Vaux led an archaeological expedition, organized by the Jordan Department of Antiquities, to the Wadi Qumran. They dug some trial trenches and excavated two tombs but found little of interest. It was not until 1951 that they returned to make a more thorough excavation. They worked there for five seasons and completely uncovered the site of what was undoubtedly the monastery in which the scrolls had been written.

What emerged from their digging amazed everybody – a very ancient stone building containing from twenty to thirty rooms and thirteen cisterns for water. The main building was nearly forty yards long and thirty yards wide, its stone squares were covered with plaster and the floor was paved with pebbles. Palm trunks and clay-covered reeds had made the roof. Some of the rooms could be identified as the dining-room or refectory, the kitchen, a potter's workshop,

60

store rooms and a scriptorium: a room in which manuscripts were written and copied. In the scriptorium were the scattered remains of a long table, and there were two ink-wells, one of bronze and the other of clay. They were like the non-spill type we use today, and one of them contained dried ink made of lamp black and gum. It was the same kind of ink as that used for the cave manuscripts!

At the north-west corner of the monastery was a two-story tower, probably used for defense, and underneath it was a store house. In the kitchen there was an oven and a hole in the wall for a flue; in the dining-room about a thousand jars and bowls were neatly arrayed in piles against the walls. Another long room had a stone platform at one end that might have been a pulpit. The potter's workshop contained a round group of stones which held the potter's wheel. There were lamps, nails, locks and keys, and iron tools such as scythes and pruning knives lying around. A very important find was a jar which was exactly the same shape as the jars in which the first scrolls were found. There were potsherds – pieces of broken pottery – and the letters on them matched the writing on the manuscripts. Here was proof that the monastery and the cave manuscripts belonged to the same time and the same people.

Steps led down to the six large cisterns which supplied the inhabitants of the monastery with water. In the rainy season they would have to store all the water they could to last for the rest of the year. On the surface level were seven smaller cisterns which may have been used for baptisms.

At some time an earthquake had weakened the tower, cracked one of the cisterns and caused ceilings to collapse, and a layer of ashes indicates that the monastery was later destroyed by fire. The ashes contained the charred and blackened remains of the reeds and palm trunks which had formed the roof.

When more of the tombs in the cemetery, which lay between the monastery and the sea, were opened it was found that all the bodies had been buried in the same way, face upwards with the head to the south. They had not been placed in coffins but in a small room at the bottom of a trench. On the surface the graves were marked by two upright stones, with pebbles in between them. There were no pots, urns or tools in the graves, everything was as simple as it could possibly be. Skeletons of both men and women were found.

Who were these people who had lived in the monastery? Father de Vaux, and many other scholars believe that they were members of a religious sect called Essenes (mentioned

by Pliny) who gathered there for work, meals, prayers and meetings, and who lived in the caves, under tents or in huts at the foot of the cliffs. When they died they were laid side by side in the near-by cemetery.

Their life would have been hard as the region was poor in natural resources, had a scanty rainfall and a very hot climate. They would probably have fields in the more fertile plain at the top of the cliff, and their cattle, sheep and goats would graze in the mountains.

In 1958 Father de Vaux made further excavations near the spring of Ain Feshkha, two miles south of Khirbet Qumran, and discovered what may have been a farm belonging to the community. He found a large building with storage sheds, several pools or vats connected by narrow channels which may have been used for preparing leather, enclosures for animals, and a shed that was perhaps used for drying dates.

The Essenes were Jews who had cut themselves off from the official religion of the priests of the Temple at Jerusalem, and from the other two major Jewish sects, the Pharisees and Sadducees. They were a brotherhood of people working and living together in communities such as the one at Qumran. They believed in self-control and discipline, obedience and holiness, and gave up all pleasures and worldly goods, sharing all possessions. They observed the Sabbath very strictly but did not believe in animal sacrifices. They had withdrawn from the world and all its temptations, and had adopted a life of simplicity and hard work in order to find freedom in fellowship and in practising their religion the way they wanted to.

What we know of the Essenes comes chiefly from the Jewish historian Josephus, Philo from Alexandria in Egypt, and the Roman Pliny, who all lived in the first century A.D. when the Essenes were flourishing and the members of the Qumran community were studying and copying their manuscripts. These three writers all tell us different things about the Essenes, and sometimes they contradict each other, but the accounts they give tally in many ways with the information gathered from the scrolls, and especially from the one called the Manual of Discipline. The arguments among scholars will go on for a long time, but it is fairly safe to say that the people of Qumran, if not Essenes or a branch of the order, belonged to the same general type and had a strong connection with them or with other Jewish groups who lived an Essenic kind of life.

The excavations at Qumran brought to light some hundreds of coins, some of them in pots, some just lying around. Now coins with inscriptions on them, or heads of kings or emperors, are much easier to find a date for than most things

that are dug up from the earth, and if they have an actual date on them the task of the archaeologist is made quite simple. Some of the coins had been in use over a hundred years B.C. and others were as late as A.D. 135. From this evidence, as well as from the pottery, the earthquake and the fire, scholars have been able to build up a picture of what happened to the monastery and its inhabitants. It has had to be skilfully put together like a very difficult jigsaw puzzle, and though some of the pieces are still missing we now have a good idea, not only of the day to day life in the community, but also when it began and ended, why the scrolls were hidden in the caves, and why they remained undiscovered for nearly two thousand years.

There were three main periods in the history of Khirbet Qumran. The coins found at the deepest levels indicate that the first building was done in the reign of John Hyrcanus (135–104 B.C.) and first occupied during the reign of Alexander Jannaeus (104–78 B.C.). These two men were members of the great Asmonaean family which provided the Jews with a number of priest-kings, delivered them from the power of the Syrians and brought them to greatness again after hundreds of years of subjection. From 78 B.C. the Essenic sect went peaceably about its affairs up to the year

A.D. 68, except for a time when the building was damaged by an earthquake. This happened, according to Josephus, in the seventh year of the reign of Herod the Great, in the spring of 31 B.C., when all Judaea was shaken and thirty thousand people were killed. The members of the community evidently moved out and did not return for thirty years, and we do not know why they stayed away for all that time. When they did return they had to make major repairs to the building, reinforce the tower and strengthen the walls.

A second sequence of coins ends at A.D. 68, the second year of a revolt by the Jews against the Romans. The rebellion failed and after it was over the commander-in-chief of the Roman army, Vespasian, left a garrison of soldiers in Jericho, which he had captured, only seven miles away from Qumran, and it is clear that the Roman forces attacked the monastery and destroyed it. The destruction was much greater than that of the earthquake nearly a hundred years before. The layers of black ash, the broken walls and a number of arrow-heads are all evidence of a great battle and the total defeat of the few defenders who had stayed in the tower.

The building was abandoned forever by the Essenes. Most of them had probably left before the final destruction when they realized the danger from the approaching Roman forces. What became of them we do not know. They disappear from

history. But before they disappeared they put the scrolls that made up their library into jars and hid them in the most inaccessible caves they could find, hoping, no doubt, that they would be able to return some time and recover their precious possessions when the fighting was over. But they never did so and never again do we hear of the community of Qumran.

The ruins of the monastery were, for a time, occupied by the Romans and used as a post for watching and guarding the shore of the Dead Sea. Coins have been found from the reigns of Nero, Titus and Herod Agrippa II, but the military occupation does not seem to have lasted beyond about A.D. 86.

Then there is silence from Qumran until the year A.D. 132. In that year a second Jewish revolt against the Romans broke out and lasted for three years. For a short time during this period the Jewish rebels used Khirbet Qumran as a strong point protecting the Dead Sea route to their southern outposts. Fourteen Roman coins and one Jewish coin struck by Simeon, one of the leaders of the rebellion, have been found.

After the rebels had been crushed in A.D. 135 the only visitors to Qumran were a few wandering shepherds, and the silence of the desert hung heavily over the ruins of a once busy community.

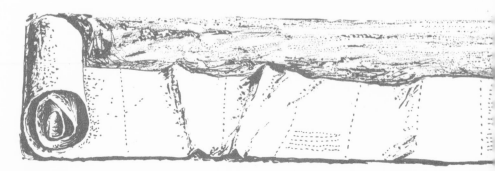

Chapter Seven

IT IS TIME now to turn to the scrolls themselves and find out why they are of such importance that many books have been written about them, and many fierce arguments carried on between scholars about what the contents reveal.

The scrolls are in manuscript: that is, they are written by hand. They are not original compositions as far as we know, but are more likely to be copies, or copies made from another copy, or copies made from a long series of copyings. The Bedouins took eleven scrolls or parts of scrolls from the Qumran cave in 1947. Six of them are separate compositions, but one of them is in two versions. Therefore we speak of the seven Dead Sea Scrolls of the first discovery.

Two of the scrolls contain the Book of Isaiah from the Old Testament. One of them was bought by the Archbishop Samuel and is in an almost perfect condition. It is made of strips of leather stitched at the edges. All the sixty-six chapters are there, most of them intact, in fifty-four columns of writing. The other Book of Isaiah, bought by Professor Sukenik, was in a bad state of preservation. Much of the leather had rotted away and it could hardly be unrolled. But there is

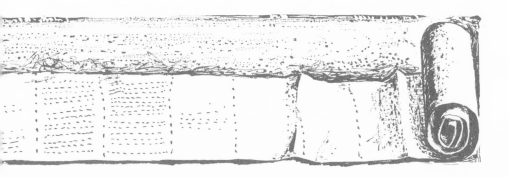

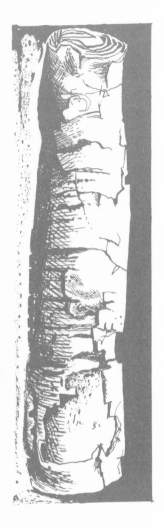

enough of the text left for it to be studied. It contains most of chapters thirty-eight to sixty-six, and parts of some of the earlier chapters.

The Qumran manuscripts of Isaiah are many hundreds of years older than any other Hebrew manuscript of that book in existence. That in itself is exciting, even though the original book was written hundreds of years earlier than the cave scrolls. All our manuscripts of the Hebrew Old Testament contain the text as it was corrected and edited from ancient writings during the first centuries A.D. This was done by Jewish scholars called Masoretes, and we call the text the Masoretic text. The cave scrolls are, then, pre-Masoretic.

Careful examination of the Isaiah scrolls shows that there are many minor differences from the Masoretic text we read in our Bible; not only changes in spelling and grammar, but there are also additions and omissions. But there are no startling differences which alter the meaning of the text of Isaiah. On the whole the wording is much the same as that of the Masoretes. Professor Sukenik's manuscript is closer to the Masoretic text than the Archbishop's, which probably means that it is not so old.

When Jesus unrolled the parchment Book of Isaiah in the synagogue at Nazareth one Sabbath and read from it, the words would be very similar to those of the Dead Sea Scroll.

70

Isaiah was a major prophet, but we call Habakkuk a minor prophet, and the Book of Habakkuk in the Old Testament is very short, consisting of only three chapters. But it is beautifully written, a model of literary composition. One of the Dead Sea Scrolls was a commentary on the first two chapters of this book. It is about five feet long and less than six inches wide. The beginning is missing but its general condition is good. The author quoted verses from Habakkuk and added his own explanation of their meaning. Unfortunately for us, his comments are so vague that it is often difficult for scholars to understand whether the persons and events he mentions belong to his past, present or future, and this has led to a great deal of confusion in trying to identify them.

The writer often speaks of a wicked priest who persecutes a righteous teacher, and of a false prophet. Who the Teacher of Righteousness was is not known. We can only guess, and almost every scholar has guessed a different name. It is likely that he was once the leader of the community of Qumran, or its founder, or perhaps the title refers to a rank in the community held by different people at different times, and not to a particular person. More evidence is needed before he can be given a name, but this will not prevent more books being written trying to prove that he was this man, that man

or the other. Scholars, like the rest of us, get led away by their interest and enthusiasm, and are as likely as less learned people to make wild guesses and then twist the evidence they have to make it fit in with their guess.

A similar difficulty has arisen over the identity of the Wicked Priest. One man who has been considered a strong possibility is Alexander Jannaeus, the Priest-King of the Jews from 104–78 B.C. He persecuted religious groups in Judaea and had a lust for power and conquest. He added many Gentile cities to his kingdom, and made himself rich with the treasures he plundered from them.

The Manual of Discipline, also from the Archbishop's collection, is the manuscript which had become separated into two scrolls. Joined together the scrolls would be six feet long and nearly ten inches wide. Again, the beginning is missing, and the leather is of a coarser quality than that of the other scrolls. It is sometimes given the title The Order of the Community.

The first part of the manuscript describes a covenant, or contract, of steadfast love in which the members of the community are united with God. Then there is an account of the two spirits in man, one of light and truth, the other darkness and falsehood. Then follow the rules of the community, and it ends with a long psalm of thanksgiving.

The Manual of Discipline tells us a lot about the daily life

72

of the Essenic sect living at Qumran; how new members were admitted, of the standard of conduct they had to live up to, and the rules they had to keep. They had to practise the truth, along with modesty, justice and righteousness, to love piety, and to work humbly in all their ways.

The Essenes did not believe in private property. When they joined the order they gave all their possessions to it, and then held all their belongings in common. They wore white garments, they believed that baptism in water would cleanse them from sin, and that the soul would live for ever.

Children had to study for ten years before they could become members at the age of twenty. If they passed the test they were put on a year's probation, and were only fully enrolled after another year, when they swore an oath of allegiance.

Every member of the community was given a special rank, and could be either promoted or demoted by a vote taken among the members. They ate together after the priest had blessed the food. Everyone sat in order of rank, the priest in the first place. They met together regularly for prayer and study. Indeed, each member had to spend one third of the nights of the year studying with his companions.

73

If a member broke one of the rules he was isolated from his fellows for a number of days or weeks, or even for a year. Sometimes he was not allowed to have his rations. If he repeated his offenses he was liable to be expelled for good and would have to return to the outside world as a failure. The rules were very strict, and there were many of them. There were penalties for such things as indulging in raucous laughter, going to sleep in a meeting, interrupting a neighbor's speaking, and to take the name of God in vain was a terrible sin.

A very well-preserved scroll from the collection of Professor Sukenik is The War of the Sons of Light with the Sons of Darkness, sometimes called simply The Rule of War. It is about nine feet long and six inches wide. It describes a conflict between the good and the wicked, but does not seem to be the story of a war that actually happened. It is probably a prophecy of the future as the writer imagined it, when the end of the world would come and God's Kingdom would be established.

In this mysterious war the armies were divided into groups of tens, fifties, hundreds and thousands, and were made up of foot and horse soldiers, archers, slingers and charioteers. One section of the scroll describes military maneuvers, trumpet signals, directions for hurling stones and slinging javelins, and another deals with banners and their inscriptions.

The scroll forecasts that at the end of days each side would win three times in turn, but at the end of the seventh campaign the great hand of God would bring final victory to the Sons of Light — whom we take to be the people of Israel. Everlasting righteousness would then be brought in and the Kingdom of God would last for ever.

The Thanksgiving Psalms, also from the Sukenik collection, were in four bundles, three of them crushed together, and the fourth was very difficult to open. The pieces of leather are about thirteen inches wide. The scroll contains parts of twenty psalms, similar to the psalms in the Old Testament, but on the whole not such good ones. They give thanks to God for His goodness, and most of them begin with the words. "I give thanks unto Thee, O Lord."

Another scroll was, when first found, given the wrong name. The word "Lamech" was deciphered on a fragment of the scroll before the leather could be softened and unrolled without injury, and it was thought that it might turn out to be the lost Book of Lamech, a work mentioned in one or two ancient lists but never before seen. So it was called the Lamech Scroll. But when it was unrolled in 1956 it was found to contain chapters five to fifteen from the Book of Genesis, in which two Lamechs are mentioned. One was a descendant of Cain, and the other the father of Noah.

75

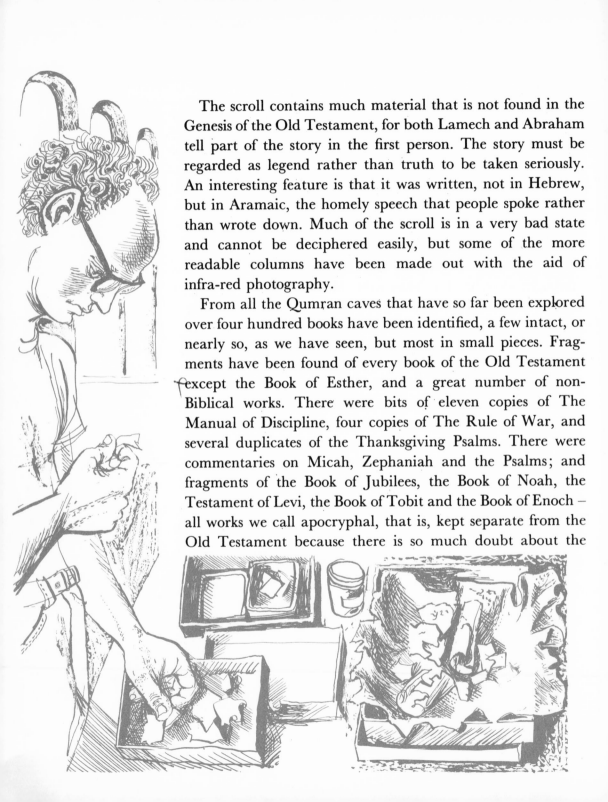

The scroll contains much material that is not found in the Genesis of the Old Testament, for both Lamech and Abraham tell part of the story in the first person. The story must be regarded as legend rather than truth to be taken seriously. An interesting feature is that it was written, not in Hebrew, but in Aramaic, the homely speech that people spoke rather than wrote down. Much of the scroll is in a very bad state and cannot be deciphered easily, but some of the more readable columns have been made out with the aid of infra-red photography.

From all the Qumran caves that have so far been explored over four hundred books have been identified, a few intact, or nearly so, as we have seen, but most in small pieces. Fragments have been found of every book of the Old Testament except the Book of Esther, and a great number of non-Biblical works. There were bits of eleven copies of The Manual of Discipline, four copies of The Rule of War, and several duplicates of the Thanksgiving Psalms. There were commentaries on Micah, Zephaniah and the Psalms; and fragments of the Book of Jubilees, the Book of Noah, the Testament of Levi, the Book of Tobit and the Book of Enoch – all works we call apocryphal, that is, kept separate from the Old Testament because there is so much doubt about the genuineness of their contents.

There are tens of thousands of these scraps, some as big as a hand, some containing only a single letter. They have to go through a long and delicate process of being cleaned, unfolded, smoothed out and placed between sheets of glass. They are mostly of leather, only a few are papyrus. They range in color from blackish-brown to the paleness of paper. If they have turned quite black they are photographed with infra-red rays, and writing that the naked eye cannot see is brought to light. The men working on them give a sigh of relief when they come across a piece on which the writing is beautifully clear!

When all this preliminary work is done the fragments have to be pieced together, and the bits from the same book sorted out, and this is the most gigantic jigsaw puzzle that the world has ever known. It is being gradually solved in the Palestine Archaeological Museum in the old part of Jerusalem, in a long room nicknamed the Scrollery. Father de Vaux presides over this work, and two of his chief helpers are Father Milik, a Roman Catholic priest from Poland, and John Allegro of Manchester University. It may take from ten to fifty years to sort out all the thousands of scraps and decipher them.

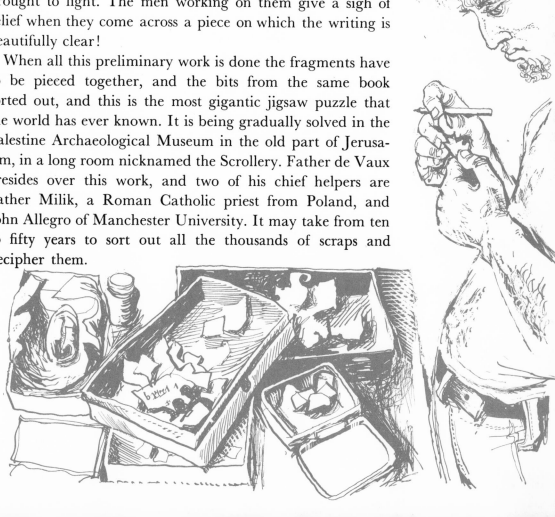

Chapter Eight

IT WILL BE interesting now to hear more about the discoveries at the Wadi Murabba'at caves, mentioned briefly in Chapter Four, and to learn what connection they have with the more famous findings from Qumran.

The Wadi Murabba'at lies about eleven miles south of Qumran and eighteen miles south-east of Jerusalem. It is a great gorge, sheer on its north side and sloping steeply on the south, and when it reaches the Dead Sea its sides are almost vertical. Early in 1952 some Bedouin of the Ta'amire tribe were offering for sale pieces of leather with Hebrew and Greek writing on them. When the archaeological authorities of Jordan heard about this, and where they had come from, they at once instituted their own search, under Mr G. L. Harding and Father de Vaux, taking Bedouin guides along with them. When they arrived at the caves on the north side of the gorge they found to their surprise that there were already a large number of the tribesmen hard at work at their own illegal excavations. Some of these were kept on with the official expedition and various caves were explored. The party pitched their tents on a narrow ledge of rock at the

79

foot of the cliff, but they soon discovered that it was not a good choice. When it rained the water, streaming down the slope, washed large boulders away and sent them crashing into the camp. One member narrowly escaped being hit by a rock as it fell on the bed from which he had just moved away.

There was also danger in the caves from collapsing roofs, dust filled the air and put out the pressure lamps, and the excavators had to use kerosene flares instead. These gave off a smoke which made it difficult to breathe. Later, however, the Arab Legion came to the rescue with a portable generator, and though this made the work somewhat easier the men were working under great difficulties all the time.

Their excavations showed that the caves had been used by man for thousands of years, right back to between 4,000 and 3,000 B.C. In layers of earth and stones were found flint tools, javelin heads and bone instruments. But the most remarkable finds were some wooden objects, preserved by being protected from the weather and the heat in the deep recesses of the caves. One was the haft of an adze, a tool used by farmers and carpenters. The head was shaped like an axe but was hafted with the cutting edge at right angles to the line of the handle. This adze was complete with polished handle and leather thongs, looking as new as though it had been made the day before.

From another layer in the same cave came some remains of a Bronze Age settlement — about 2000 to 1550 B.C. There were bronze needles, an alabaster vase and pieces of pottery.

In three of the caves there were remains of Iron Age men who had lived there in the seventh or eighth centuries B.C., but it was their occupation in Roman times that provided most articles – pottery, lamps, bronze heads of picks and javelins, iron arrowheads, knives, nails and needles, and even a key! There were bowls and plates of wood, combs, buttons, spoons, the remains of clothing and sandals, and coins. Most of the coins came from the period of the Second Jewish Revolt of A.D. 132–135.

Written documents were found from the last three periods. From the Iron Age, when the last Kings of Judah were reigning, came a papyrus palimpsest in Phoenician writing, which seems to be a list of names and numbers written over a letter. (A palimpsest is writing material which has been used a second time after the original writing has been erased.)

From the Arab period came some paper documents in Arabic. But from the Roman period again came the most important material – letters, legal documents, a marriage contract, pieces of pottery, and fragments of Biblical manuscripts written in Hebrew on leather. These included four

scrolls, the Book of Genesis, two of Exodus, and one of Deuteronomy. At some time they had all been roughly torn to pieces, perhaps by a Roman soldier. Other manuscripts had been nibbled by rats and used to line their nests.

The Second Jewish Revolt against the Romans has already been mentioned. It took place from A.D. 132–135, when Hadrian was the Roman Emperor. Simeon, the leader of the revolt, called himself Prince of Israel. Some people believed that he was the expected Messiah, but Jewish Christians called him an impostor because they believed that Jesus had been the Messiah the world had waited for. Simeon fought fiercely against the Romans, and it took three years before his rebellion was crushed. Some of the documents found in the Wadi Murabba'at caves showed that one of Simeon's garrisons was stationed there, under the command of Joshua Ben-Galgolah. Two letters to Joshua from his leader were among the finds. One of them said: "From Simeon Ben-Kosebah to Joshua Ben-Galgolah and the men of your company. Greetings! I call heaven to witness against me that if any one of the Galileans whom you have protected causes trouble I will put fetters on your feet as I did to Ben Aflul. Simeon Ben-Kosebah, Prince of Israel." We can only guess what the unhappy Ben-Aflul had done to incur the wrath of Simeon!

Other caves in the neighborhood of Murabba'at produced more manuscripts in fragmentary form — a letter to Simeon from another of his garrisons, pieces of Old Testament books, a column of a Greek copy of the Book of Habakkuk and a scroll of the Minor Prophets in Hebrew, belonging to the second century A.D. and very close to the Masoretic text. The Minor Prophet scroll has suffered through damp and has become blackened by age, and only infra-red photography shows any writing on it at all.

Another hidden store of documents was discovered in 1952 at Khirbet Mird, midway between the Wadi Qumran and the Wadi Murabba'at, where another watercourse runs down to the Dead Sea, and again it was the Bedouins who started the search. They had burrowed into an underground chamber of a ruined monastery and found some papyrus fragments written in Greek and Arabic, a letter written by a Christian monk, and a fragment of a Greek play. All these are of a much later date than the Qumran and Murabba'at finds, dating from the fifth to the ninth centuries A.D. when the monastery was destroyed. One of the letters was from a man called Gabriel to the head of the monastery, asking that prayers should be offered for him in his troubles, which seem to have been connected with Arab raiders, and on account of whom, he said, "my heart is trembling."

These discoveries have no direct connection with the Qumran scrolls but they are very important because, knowing definitely that some of them were written in the second century A.D., we can be certain that the Qumran manuscripts are earlier. The Hebrew and Aramaic writing of the Murabba'at documents is of a later style than those of Qumran, and the texts of the Bible books are closer to the Masoretic texts. This means that the theory that the Qumran scrolls are earlier than the second century is very much strengthened.

Chapter Nine

EVER SINCE THE first Dead Sea Scrolls were discovered men have been asking questions about them. Have they got anything to do with Christianity? Were the Essenes connected with the first Christians? Was there a connection between the Essenes and John the Baptist? Do the scrolls throw any light on the times in which Jesus lived? Do they throw any light on Jesus himself?

Many scholars have rushed in with their theories and answers, but when so much of the picture is still missing it is dangerous to attempt to give definite answers. Some of the early statements made by scholars in a hurry have been shown to be wrong, and much more evidence is needed before anyone can say with certainty what, if anything, the Essenic sect of Qumran had to do with Christianity. The scrolls only give us confusing hints.

They do, however, add greatly to our knowledge of the religious background of the New Testament. They give us a picture of what life was like in the times when John the Baptist was preaching in the wilderness and baptizing those who believed that the Kingdom of Heaven was at hand. They give us information about a religious organization which was in existence during Jesus' lifetime, the members of which looked upon themselves as the true Israel, the chosen people of God. They believed that the end of their age was near, and that a new world was about to dawn under an expected Messiah. Some of their ideas were adopted by the early Christian Church, but there is no trace in any of the scrolls of the things that Jesus taught that made Christianity so different from any other religion.

The Essenes were in no sense Christians at any time during which the sect was flourishing, and they did not believe in any of the ideas that make up the Christian faith. There is nothing in their writings so far discovered about a Saviour who suffered, was crucified, and rose again, and no description of any Christian practices.

There are many phrases and ideas in the Qumran rules which resemble phrases and ideas in the New Testament, but there are also many which are found in the writings of other sects of those days, sects which had no connection with Christianity. This is further proof that it is not wise to say, as some writers have done, that the Essenic beliefs developed into Christianity of their own accord. If that had been the case Jesus would not have been necessary, and the Gospels need not have been written. It is possible that John the

Baptist may have known of the people of the monastery, may perhaps have lived with them for a time and adopted some of their ideas. When Jesus came, however, he brought a new way of life and a new promise for the future that the Essenes had known nothing about, and would not have agreed with if they had.

The men of Qumran kept themselves apart from the world, but Jesus mixed with good men and bad men, with rich and poor. Jesus proclaimed the gift of eternal life for all. The men of the community believed that only they would inherit salvation. The teachings of Jesus are part of our lives today, whereas the Essenes disappeared from history when their work was done and their usefulness had come to an end. One might say that the beliefs of the Essenes were a link between Judaism and the Christian Church. The scrolls show that there was much unrest among religious people in the years just before the birth of Christ, and that men were examining and questioning the basic ideas of the Jewish faith. The Qumran men turned to rigidity and exclusiveness. Christianity brought inspiration and revolution. Essenism, Judaism and Christianity sprang from a common ground of Old Testament beliefs. They borrowed from each other, and one cannot be understood without the others, yet they became three separate and distinct movements.

One great value of the Dead Sea Scrolls is the chance they give us to compare the many different translations of the Bible and check their accuracy. Up till 1947 we had Greek translations of 285 B.C. to 150 B.C., though not the actual manuscripts, Aramaic translations of the second century A.D., and Latin translations of about the year A.D. 400. These are different from the Masoretic text and from each other. Now that the very much older text of Isaiah is available the translation which is closest to it is likely to be more accurate in all the other books of the Bible.

The scrolls are also of great interest to the experts in the history of the alphabet and of palaeography, and to students of the development of the Hebrew language. Some ancient books originally written in Hebrew have been lost for two thousand years, and only their titles have been known. Now, fragments of the Book of Tobit, the Book of Enoch and the Book of Jubilees give us a little information about their contents, and there is always the hope that more may be found somewhere in the Dead Sea region.

We must be content at the moment with the little we can be certain about. The quest for the scrolls has brought interest, excitement and jubilation to the men who found them, to those who worked to put them together and made their contents known, and to the thousands of people who have read about them and have eagerly followed one of the greatest mystery stories of all time.

Muhammad the Wolf is a man now. Perhaps he has forgotten the hot spring day when a straying goat led him to the beginning of a strange adventure. Perhaps he has got what he wanted – to live in the city and drive a motor car. Or perhaps he still climbs the craggy cliffs and pokes about in holes, dreaming that one day he might find, in a dim and dusty crevice, more of the pots that brought such wonder to the world.

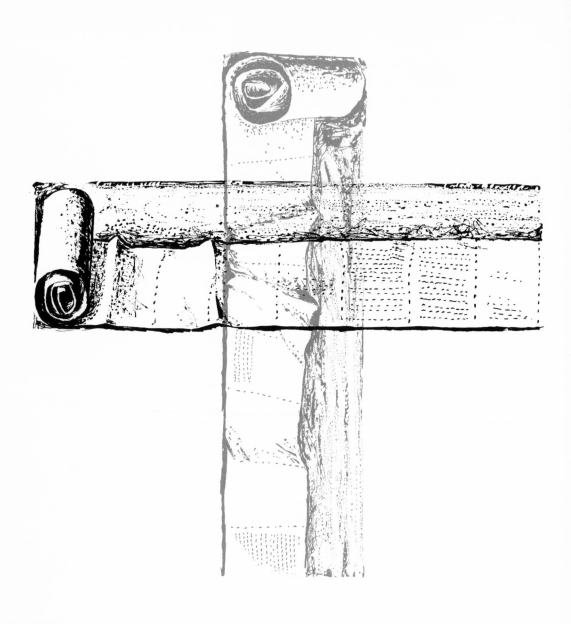

BIBLIOGRAPHY

Allegro, J. M., *The Dead Sea Scrolls*, Penguin, 1956.

———, *The People of the Dead Sea Scrolls*, Doubleday, 1958.

———, *The Treasure of the Copper Scrolls*, Doubleday, 1960.

Bruce, F. F., *Second Thoughts on the Dead Sea Scrolls*, revised edition, Wm. B. Eerdmans, 1961.

Burrows, Millar, *The Dead Sea Scrolls*, Viking, 1955.

———, *More Light on the Dead Sea Scrolls*, Viking, 1958.

Danielou, Jean, *The Dead Sea Scrolls and Primitive Christianity*, New American Library, 1962.

Davies, A. Powell, *The Meaning of the Dead Sea Scrolls*, New American Library, 1956.

Eisenberg, Azriel, *The Great Discovery*, Abelard-Schuman, 1956.

Fritsch, Charles T., *The Qumran Community*, Macmillan Company, New York, 1956.

Gaster, Theodor H., *The Dead Sea Scriptures*, Doubleday, 1956.

Schonfield, Hugh J., *Secrets of the Dead Sea Scrolls*, Peter Smith, 1962.

Van der Ploeg, J., *The Excavations at Qumran*, Longmans, Green, 1958.

Vermes, G., *The Dead Sea Scrolls in English*, Peter Smith, 1963.

Wilson, Edmund, *The Scrolls from the Dead Sea*, Oxford University Press, 1955.

INDEX

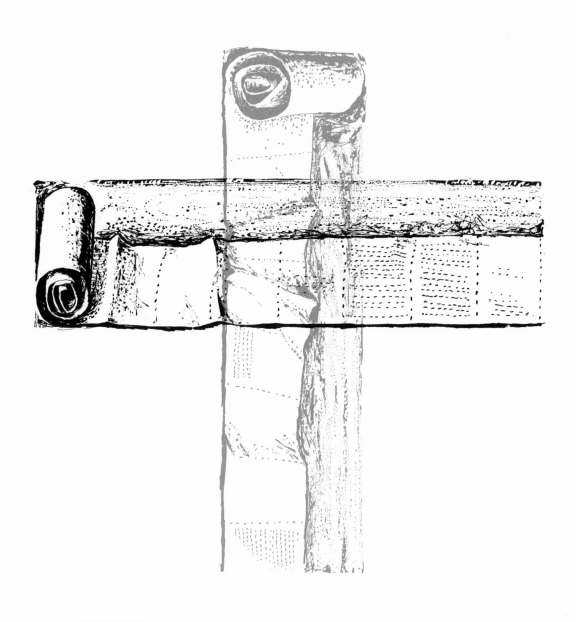

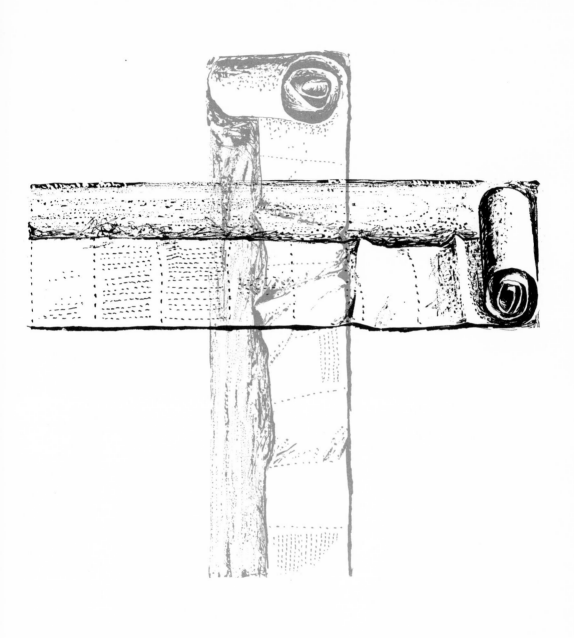

About the Author

GEOFFREY PALMER spent his childhood in the Robin Hood country around Sherwood Forest in Nottinghamshire, England. He is now the Headmaster of a large primary school in London.

Mr. Palmer is interested in archaeology and folklore and has written several books on these subjects. His other interests include opera-going, collecting gramophone records and browsing in secondhand bookshops, the dustier the better.